Change Machine

Jaya Savige was born in Sydney, raised on Bribie Island, and lives in London. He is the author of *Latecomers* (UQP, 2005), which won the New South Wales Premier's Prize for Poetry and was highly commended for the ASAL Mary Gilmore Award, and *Surface to Air* (UQP, 2011), which was shortlisted for *The Age* Poetry Book of the Year and the Western Australian Premier's Book Award for Poetry. He read for a PhD on James Joyce at the University of Cambridge (Christ's) as a Gates Scholar, and has held Australia Council residencies at the B.R. Whiting Studio, Rome, and the Cité Internationale des Arts, Paris. He lectures at the New College of the Humanities at Northeastern, and is poetry editor for *The Australian*.

Also by Jaya Savige

Latecomers
Surface to Air
Maze Bright

F
oR

J
O
H
N,

Il Miglior Fabbro.

Jaya **Savige**

Change Machine

[signature]

OCTOBER 2022

UQP

First published 2020 by University of Queensland Press
PO Box 6042, St Lucia, Queensland 4067 Australia

uqp.com.au
reception@uqp.uq.edu.au

Cover design by Sandy Cull, www.sandycull.com
Author photograph provided by the author
Typeset in 11/14 pt Bembo Std by Post Pre-press Group, Brisbane
Printed in Australia by McPherson's Printing Group

  The University of Queensland Press is
assisted by the Australian Government
through the Australia Council, its arts
funding and advisory body.

A catalogue record for this book is available from the National Library of Australia.

ISBN 978 0 7022 6286 9 (pbk)
ISBN 978 0 7022 6420 7 (pdf)

University of Queensland Press uses papers that are natural, renewable
and recyclable products made from wood grown in well-managed forests.
The logging and manufacturing processes conform to the environmental
regulations of the country of origin.

for my fathers
and my son

Contents

There There

Machine, or Engine, in Mechanicks, is whatsoever hath Force sufficient either to raise or stop the Motion of a Body.

—John Harris, *Lexicon Technicum* (1704)

Mean Time Between Failures

ROTFLMAOWTRDMF

Egypt hasn't had a native king since Nekhtnebf
held out at Memphis
against the Persians, then his nephew
didn't. But even that wait seems no more excessive

than yours. Engineers measure the average life
expectancy of a system by the Mean Time Between Failures (MTBF).
(Working backwards, then, from Brexit to Suez,
Westminster needs an oil change about every seventy years.)

Replays show a peloton, summoning the dregs of oomph,
grow tangled in the thirty elbows of itself
before crashing into the base of the Arc de Triomphe,

when—finally!—your jacket pocket vibrates with a kiss,
and the emoji for *rolling on the floor laughing my ass off*
with tears running down my face.

The Endeavour

Flushed, hopeful, awkward as a spaceman,
he opens the chute and pushes his specimen
jar into it.

Before letting go, he clings to it
for a second, as though it were the last vitamin
on a research vessel riddled with scurvy and vermin.

His senses are haywire: wafts of jasmine and pine
weave with clove, boot leather and semen.
The aircon hums, a hive, a theremin.

Now he is climbing the *Endeavour*'s mast.
He scales the rigging like a salt, right to the crow's nest,
where he camps. For long nights, with chapped lips,

he sleeps with one eye peeled to a microscope
for the islands of a blastocyst.

The Cobra of Djemma el Fna

Neither of us mentioned your weight loss
the morning we left Marrakech
at sun-up and rode hard for the High Atlas.
I cannot remember which miscarriage

that was after, which sounds thoughtless,
but I am trying to get how, in your bathrobe,
you said you were saddened by the cobra
'dancing' in Djemma el Fna—

and so, to lighten the load, I played at Hefner
(then the part where we were weightless),
and afterwards I took you to the best hammam
in the capital for a proper scrub with cardamom.

Now I am trying to get how the Berber village
at dusk seemed to us as soundless
as the town that banned dancing in *Footloose*.
Sometimes my attempts are fruitless.

Give It a Rest, Mr Fowler

The harshest and least necessary bit of literary
criticism I have read is in the *Dictionary
of National Biography*. It was written by one 'T.F.',
Thomas Fowler, his victim Edmund Staunton.

I knew the text in question. After collecting our little one
in his hard cardboard cylinder
that now graces our mantelpiece, despite being irreligious,

we scraped through frigid wind into a house
of God on the banks of the river.

There, a brass plaque changed us. Which is why I fume (*WTF?*)
when I read in the *DNB* again:

> *Ten of Staunton's children lie buried in Kingston
> church, where a brass over their grave
> commemorates the fact* [and if he had any shame
> he would have left it there] *in doggerel rhyme.*

Rimbaud in Salatiga

*Let us not try to find out whether the poet who wanted
one day to 'steal fire' sold one thing rather than another.*
                                                    —Yves Bonnefoy

This is how the world ends:
      with strange foliage, *ficus* and tamarinds,
and one they call the flame-of-the-forest. Java.
      The night we docked in sweltering Batavia,

      I thought of Verne, and winced—
how had the *Twenty Thousand Leagues* ever convinced
      me I had known the archipelago of stars,
the million golden birds? You dwindle, my blind jongleurs

of debauchery, your silks bedim to alamode
      beside the proper miracle of Suez.
The wind that called my name off the coast of Abyssinia

jangles these jujubes, too: *You are someone else. Any business
will do: coffee, explosives, the slave trade, the circus.*
    The muse can get another Ganymede.

Fiona in Victoria Says

according to her handspan on the screen,
an Uber from Gozleme's in Melbourne
to Kakadu

would set you back as much as one from Lisbon
to Istanbul; Newcastle to Perth, Tehran

to Kathmandu;
while Bunbury to Cooktown far outstrips Boston
to the Caymans. There is a decent chance

Great Britain fits seven times in Queensland,

and three Northern Irelands
could squeeze into the Bight—the aperture
below the Nullarbor—

with her thumb near to Dublin, South Australia,
and her pinkie stretching to Esperance.

I was Driving North to Woombye

on what is now the Steve Irwin Way,
but was then the Glass House Mountains Road,

when I beamed a juvenile tiger quoll
feasting on tartare of cane toad
                              in a blaze of sclerophyll

like something out of a romantic zombie
comedy filmed in Gympie.

Now I think of the pine plantations of Beerburrum
as a between-space—a *Zwischenraum*

            where carnivorous undead Bambi
creep up on doomed young romantics in their kombi
vans: dreamcatchers swaying, Rachmaninoff

surging as we slow zoom through the moonroof.

Toodaloo

Tonight as we were drying the dishes
at our hovel in the fourth arrondissement,
you remarked how that bird from Mauritius,
      the dodo, became an icon of extinction

      only because Alice Liddell
loved the stuffed specimen at the Ashmolean
so much that the indecently smitten Carroll
      revivified it in *Alice's Adventures.*

'It also survives as a watermark on Mauritian
cash,' you added, 'but the Oxford one was reduced to ashes
by curators, due to soft-tissue deterioration.'

Then it clicked: my late nan's word for 'farewell'—*Toodaloo*—
must have been the Greatest Generation's
                  Franglais *à tout à l'heure.*

Yuki's Replacement

                                had a motion sensor.
This allowed it to detect if you were near,

but not if you were far. You could trip its bark
by dropping a slinky into the sensor's arc.
It was fun to trigger that mechanical yap.

But Nan did not name it. So when I try to list,
for my son, the pets I've known by name,
I'm at a loss: Heidi, Scruffy, Bernie, Yuki ... *blip*.

Before she died, I studied their affection in the dim
                curtained fortress of her flat on the coast.

                By the ambient warmth of the fridge
                        she expertly wove
                        in and out of reach
                        of her nameless love.

Whatever the Question, the Cordless

leaf blower is his answer most Sundays. Ergonomic, instant start, cruise
control—it's optimal for managing a plot.

      It works a dream

      for purging light

debris, but comes into its own in turbo mode, with soggy cuttings, sods
and rotting limes. He works in bursts, strafing the drive with
semiautomatic jets, and in the rests day's quietude pathetically returns

like a wallaby cradled in a fire blanket. He is there still, wearing only the
pink briefs of dusk, herding into a nice pile the last outstanding invoice.
With one more pass he could well whisk

      the tantalising clod

      of muck that ruins

everything. Manoeuvring the nozzle, he swells the tattered shade cloth
like a god, and sails west beyond all monologue.

Elephant in a Time of Unrest
Bangkok, 2009

A live round's report is crisper than all the dialects
of two-stroke; so you could hear the commotion
from any one of the 7-Elevens at Din Daeng Junction.

Because it happened to be April 13—*Songkran*,
the cleansing festival (hoses, water pistols, buckets,
drenching even the chickens on the motor scooters)—

the shoppers flapped, disoriented. No-one, not even
the wizened elephant crossing the road into Sukhumvit,
could properly tell the sopping platoon of Super Soakers

from the troops meaning business in full combat gear.
So when the hostel lads suggested the red-light district
at Nana Plaza, I followed. I remember the Skytrain

zooming above the elephant, beyond the snake of pink
taxis, its shadow surging like the soul of traffic.

Starstruck

I cannot honestly claim to have *met* Stephen
Hawking. But once, I was skidding down the steepest
bridge in Cambridge—in the rain, on my rusting BMX,
haring into Garret Hostel Lane at the speed

of darkness—and faced a choice: plough into a murder
of gowned undergraduates on the crest
of the bend; or swerve, and be poleaxed
by a singular hackney car. I veered like a wakeboarder

     from the kerb. Grappling with the parallax,
     I slammed the brakes and tipped. Whizzing within

     touching distance of the glossy black bonnet,
     I saw it: the interstellar cockpit

     through the tint; the famous gurn, lit like jackpot
     on a Cosmic Quest slot machine.

Mirrigin

I wish I could say precisely where Yugambeh
ends and Bundjalung begins, but we only had the crumbs
of Indigenous history, local or otherwise, at school.

We were flat out distinguishing Mayor Quimby
of *The Simpsons* from Chief Quimby
of *Inspector Gadget*. And sometimes I feel like a fool

or a fraud when I speak with Sam or Tara June, or anyone
really, about the place I come from, grew up in.

We should have been told about the strychnine
at Kilcoy, the arsenic at the sheep station
of Captain Francis Griffin.

How my glow-in-the-dark cosmos might have burgeoned
even more richly in my imagination
had I known the word for stars, where I'm from, is *mirrigin*.

The Nothing

A hole would be something
              —Rockbiter

i.

Compared to The Nothing that is nowhere
yet engulfs all Fantasia
in *The NeverEnding Story*, all other celluloid villains
a child encounters seem vanilla:

none of Scar, the Queen of Hearts, Cruella de Vil,
Sid Phillips, Voldemort, Vader or Jabba
comes close to its sublime incomprehensibility
(perhaps excepting Miyazaki's No-Face and Yubaba).

Years on, you recognised the chasm
in your introductory class on French Existentialism.
Then you saw it everywhere: in Villon and Nin;
Boundary Street; an episode of *Friends*; a wind chime;

and later still, in the car park of a crematorium,
say, or a clinical waste disposal bin.

ii. (Falcor)
Thanks to Bastion, I had a decent grip on nihilism
in good time for my first orgasm.

He knew the void, the gist of entropy.

Remember when the ancient turtle sneezed,
and Atreyu blew in the swamp like a windsock,
only to learn that the oracle in the sky
he needed to get to was a squillion miles away?

Then, when quicksand took the white horse Artax,

the off-white blur in the clouds,
just the sweet rope he
needed: Falcor, the plush luckdragon, who came to impress
a generation (and who, to stop The Nothing, Bastion and
                                             all of us squeezed
as we rose, like freshly minted gods
on our way to name the Empress.)

パックマン Études

His maze was muted blue on onyx black.
We wolfed our radiance and scored some more,
then lit our guts with those. The larger wicks
could fortify our nerve to face the ghost.

For a stack of platypus at the corner store,
Pac-Man was our minotaur.

¤

A thread to Bluto? He admits it: when Toru
Iwatani pioneered the power-up,
he was plagiarising the spinach in *Popeye*.

¤

'And take your supplements,' said the osteopath.

¤

The mouth, the maze—it may have been a myth,
a ruse to raze the fear of being lost
by simulating it under controlled circumstances.

¤

White-knuckling a glowstick, he overbalances.

The Roses of Heliogabalus
Lawrence Alma-Tadema, 1888

Plugged live and wet into its socket,
the wild albino leech of my eyeball
gorges on glare, a spilt sherbet packet
fizzing in a bruised ravine of cheek.

This is what happens when you binge
on beauty: eventually the orgy kills
you—unless you happen to be the rust-
bearded pornstar with the plaited updo

downstage left, who knows to resist
the rose petals and pomegranate seeds;
or one of the contented chaise-lounge
set, boozy, oblivious in the boss's office.

But alas that's me, smothered, forsaken,
wrist to the sky, refusing to be woken.

Citicity

Even in Joyce, there is no term like, say, 'citicity' which might convey the abstract quality of 'cityness' or of being in a city …
—Richard Brown

Day-soiled, ascending the worn stairs, he thought he was still
on the escalator, subterranean again, in the crab trenches. He knew
he needed to suppress the drubbing sensation of being locked
in a physical loop, Sisyphean on a dune of fluorescent bamboo,

so tried slowing his breathing. He visualised jamming the wheel
with his briefcase, swimming out beyond the neon coral
to where a bannister of the impossible stairs shone quartz-like
in the distance. He would hike the plain hills, the fields of sorrel.

His head was next up in a row of perforations.
How he longed to glom the art of guillotining all trace
of the citicity at the threshold of his living space.

Then by chance some headlights kicked up off a hub cap, spiking
his eye like luminous anemones, or curious sea urchins.
Day-soiled, approaching the landing, he heard something tearing.

Work Do

Trending
agile
upticks
of rain
ping off
the swish
marquee,

actioning
the specifics
of some
committee
minute
on workflow
policy.

Inside, a
cascading
weir of
Prosecco
and gossip,
frizzante
banter over
dwindling
small beer:
the usual
winks and
pledges to
touch base
and urges
to float

a balloon
around the
digital space.

The simplest
escape
will always be
to ghost
through
the side flap, past
the plastic ferns
and into
the real gardens
without
a backwards
gander at
the dance floor
glittering
with outcomes.

The Monster of Whitechapel

Then word spread of the stinking blue whale–
sized cost of our carry-on. Two Wembley
pitches of rock-hard clot, some Godzilla globule
tipping a dozen double-deckers on the scales,

pulsing beneath our toes: wet wipes and muscle-
gain supplements, nappies and topical
creams for acne, condoms, hair gel, paracetamol,
cotton buds, cocaine and cooking oil.

       We kept calm and carried on,
       clutching our professionalism

       as the sun went nosing
       the ragged grey lung

       above the Gherkin
       like a pulmonary embolism.

Change Machine
Waterloo Station

London, the sky sits on your face
like the distressed arse
of a XXXL pair of stonewashed overalls.

Charity lags in the polls.
No-one escapes the advertising blitz.

London, you've done something terrible to my patience:

e.g. To take a leak I have to break
a note, and this gives me the shits.
I'm broke. And everything should be contactless.

We breathlessly await the new vaccine,
but no-one disinfects the change machine.

The turnstile
clicks like a bottle-
nose dolphin at a killer whale.   (Go on, *get in*.)

A Nice Derangement of Epitaphs

                                   'This is BBC
World Service. Violin clashes outside the Chinese embassy ...'
Mishearings are harmless; they do not embarrass
anyone, and often give you laughing spasms.

The comedic potential of malapropisms
was unlocked by Sheridan
and perfected by *Back to the Future*'s Biff Tannen
(declaring to Marty's mum: 'I'm your Density ... Destiny!').

A typo, however, can do your head in. Typos are serious.

Think of the editor's stony face
when neither spellcheck nor the subs notice
the cub reporter on the landmark IVF case
mangling the judge's ruling that *he could not condom*

such behaviour; or the paroxysm of rage as the front page
goes out (too soon?) screaming of an *Untied Kingdom.*

Unicornered

Our dinosaur balloon has lost its pep.
For weeks it commandeered the living room.
It swayed above its empire like an airship
puffing out its hull of aluminium,

taut as a kettledrum. Its bouncy arm
insisted that we recognise its thaneship
and grant its natural right to *Lebensraum*.
The old gods we were no longer to worship.

But now it slumps behind the laundry rack
for a patch and a pint of helium.
It's far too late for us to take it back

and the Co-op refuses to mend him.
The vote's already in for this month's pick:
a unicorn, declared by referendum.

You Hear It Said

                         : there are two kinds of poem.
The first extends its claws towards a bream, your uncle,
a dead pig, bare almond trees; this is the single
tractor beam, trained on your subject's sternum.

The second sniffs ahead in the so-called *ystwyth*
manner, for it winds like the river of that name.
Commencing in a cupboard you once feared,
it treads the old Silk Road to its eisteddfod.

But this division has at least one glaring problem.
It doesn't count the one we call the *boomerang*—
see how far you can fling the blooming thing

and still have it return. It can be worth
two dead pigs in your cupboard—a healthy dividend
—to reel your uncle home from Samarkand.

Uncle Robin

He was committed in twenty ten. A decade on
he finally stopped trying to impress the older inmates
(the whisky-sipping apiarist from Dundee,
the Irish naturalist, the boy wonder, the heavy breather

who took to reading Goethe on the roof
and always had a bone to pick with the Black Panthers,
and the Ulsterman, in for knifing a quoof)
with his subtle ways of unfastening the buckles

　　　　on his frazzled straitjacket—and was released.

　　　　Now he works two jobs: Maccas, and a tobacconist.
　　　　Sometimes, flipping burgers, slicing pickles,
　　　　or stocking vintage matchbooks,

　　　　he thinks of the boy wonder (naked in the kitchen,
　　　　a crown of bay leaves on his head!) and giggles.

Plunder (Business as Usual)

Can't you hear, can't you hear the thunder?
                    —Men at Work

It was never the *glow* of the women
that made me edgy, but that word: *plunder*—
the verb you use to tell us what the *men*
do, in the chorus of 'Down Under'.

Sipping Irish Breakfast, I hear the anthem
again. Start of *plum*, end of *sunder*. Wouldn't it bear
freight in your Scottish ears (like, say, *glamour*)?

It reeks of damage. Of pillage. Of the rape
scene in *Rob Roy*. The fierce rictus on Jessica Lange's
face that floors her husband (Neeson) … I wipe
the spillage. Apply pressure. Absorb *my language*.

♮

P.S. Colin, in case you think I am pulling a fast one,
I readily admit I nicked your 'Kombi-zombie' rhyme
                    for my Woombye poem
                    (but not the 'nervous-breakfast' one).

Inferno
for Chris Lilley

I seem to have a death wish.

I interrupt one of the Maroubra boys
to mock his neck tattoo of Ouroboros,
then watch his angry vein emboss
his blanched yet bulging Southern Cross.

I guess I like to make a splash.

Sometimes I don't know what comes over me.
See that bearded bloke
who looks like Ragnar Lodbrok
with a perm from circa-*Eternal Flame* Bangles?

I just informed him his leather jacket
is missing a possessive apostrophe
in the word *Hells*, to indicate the *Angels*
belong to it. ('And you don't want to imply
                            there are several Hells …')

The Keeper

Deleting surplus photos of my son
to free up memory while on the train,
I glimpse myself in 2050, wishing
I were back here, on the Northern Line,

presented with the simple choice again:
weighing up the keeper and the dud.
I fear I may have culled the richest ones—
the shattered nights he xylophoned his food,

those weeded for the seedling of a frown,
the awkward angle for his triple chin.
The manic grin collapsing like a bridge.
The earliest bonfire of his outrage.

Nor could I possibly keep these in my head
for thirty years—so set them here instead.

Infant Speech Bubble

Voice is peculiar weather, where language is
organic sausages
of air—processed
cloud meat, piped into the rennet of a breath—

and the simple truth
is Papa's words are mere indentured wind, yoked mist;
his every utterance sentences the ambling gust, the lifting fog,
to life in the moist gulag

of his lungs, where even grunts and groans are harnessed
breezes, and all his song is sky repurposed,
and the ruins of heaven
are forever rewoven,

so, watch your language buddy
up with rainbows. Ready?

The Offing

i.

On the bluff, by the lookout, off the path, in the scrub, no-one is coming
    but us. And through the coin-operated binoculars it is clear we are going
for it—in the surf, on a weekday, beyond the flags, we are creating
a little churn within the great one; and we are there again at night, conducting
    a languid choir of glowing
    phytoplankton; and we're ducking
behind the wreck, further up, where the angelfish are flashing
    in and out of the rust, and the moon wrasse nose you while egg-hunting;
and we're puffing like seal pups against a mica proscenium, edging
    toward the place where the cowrie shell's lip lies glistening,
    and the cucumbers are inching, and one is bashfully squirting;
and we're fumbling about the fire starters, the newspaper, the kindling
    because we didn't quite make it to the caravan's awning;
and we're tangled in snake vine, its bonsai persimmon dehiscing;

ii.

and we're stirring in the dunes, nude as beach beans, amid the gawping
    mauve throats of the morning
glory, ribboned with the crepe of their seedpod pith, crisping.

> And we needn't be home by evening,
> for the egret has folded the washing,
> and the shovel-nose doesn't mind ironing,
> and the rock oyster's done the recycling.

> No, we needn't come home at evening,
> for the cormorant's happily monitoring
> the little ones, and the coral is hinting
> it will soon be finished its photocopying.

So we're at it again, on elbows, knees, pawing and scooping, shovelling
    practically everything
into the bucket: handfuls of hairy cockles, sloping horse mussels, and a thing

iii.

that could have been a gold-mouthed periwinkle; and we're singing
      while connecting
the hose; and we're dancing while turning
      the tap on; and we're praising while rinsing
all kinds of Venus clam—pleated, sculpted, swollen—conceiving
  a bracelet for an imminent beach christening.

  And the veteran lifeguard is averting
  her peregrine eyes; she just keeps scanning
  the rip and triple-checking the shark netting, smirking.

    For nothing
    on Earth is distracting,
    not even the spurned cry of the lapwing;

    no nothing
    we hear is off-putting,

iv.

    not even the totalitarian yawn of the Boeing;

    and nothing
    that lurks is disturbing,
    not even the bung note of the wobbegong,

        when the shoaling wave of our toes begins curling,
        and the fetch at the pinch where it gathers is surging,
        and the tent of the shore break is cresting,
        and the firmament blurs with the ceiling.

Cocooned in our loose weave of salt, you'd think we were shimmying
    seahorse spawn, but zoom in and see: we are scrubbing
    each other like pumice, resolving
    the dilemma of skin, shirring
    a sleeve of sea, sounding
    the offing.

Biometrics

The Convict Lying Low by Hampton Court, Speaks

i.

Home is the hoof-crushed water mint,
the hard rushes, and an adamant stonechat
declaring mid-morning's parliament
again in session. I wear stag scent—oath

hosed into the osier in ample train,
chains of white-gold water like enrapt mail,
warm links aglitter in the pearl matin.

ii.

Understand: I was cold, so stole fire.
Telling you this is my one honest act.

Sometimes I squat on the palace roof, tieless,
listening to the wind riffling the loosestrife

for the vetted remains of travestied men,
the secret of the isle's foetor.

iii.

What heron consecrates a moist towelette
upon the avenue to Arethusa,
then drags its fretsome wet stiletto

across the scum, pinpointing the auras
of tadpoles? Their ripples of inept alarm.

iv.

The bowl of sky is spaffed with miso jot,
thin cottony streaks of High Wood ewes
each abashedly declaring, 'I am written'.

Since Bushy Park rolled up its winter mat,
this could be an aftershave advertisement,
and I, the Magwitch-cum-wodewose,
barefoot in the bedstraw, fixing mojitos.

Her Late Hand

Like some deathtrap whose
been earthed, the live house of her
remains unsafe. Here is mosquito
and midge language, transcribed
and there is where her
nicked a smidgen from the moon's

wiring hadn't
handwriting
din, gnat whir
and writhing;
hard tin wing
thawing rind.

Look, a whisper, *here is the*
made of a wounded

nth drawing I
hart, winding …

There must be better ways to
but this is mine: take a holograph and
over hand,
then drape it, still damp, over the
of an insect zapper. Maybe it's a
and extinction's but a glut of
a crow with comic timing in a
that only those with the

draw night in
wring it, hand
twining hard,
thin wan grid
Darwin thing
inward night,
ward, hinting
right DNA win.

Reserve your bitter myr-
Give us one last nocturne on the baby
her heaving

rh, giant wind.
grand within
writing hand.

Credo, Décor, Coder

for my sisters

i.

Past the soft twigrush, above the coral fern,
the matted yellow spikes of banksias
bend like feral corn

toward the bay. The salted ghost of Ian basks
by Buckleys Hole, daubing mozzie-coil ash
on canvas—as thumping bass, akin

to Tibrogargan (patron of his coal),
booms from a lowered Falcon's subwoofer,
swelling the painter's ad hoc sail.

To what solid thing is this web of ours
attached? To the shared credo
of midges zipping through our bower, UFOs

we casually smudge upon the décor?
To this whimbrel's corpse, an Icarus NASA
won't ever detect? Alas, the coder

stays unseen among the auras I scan—
so I gather with my blood for our sad relay
in the paltry shade of casuarinas.

ii.

Woorim's ghost crabs rallied early.
The most translucent one would be the priest,
clawing at the latest layer

of our loss. Dawn came like the dorsal stripe
of dun foals spilling newly into hay,
but could not circumvent our flood of *l'esprit*

de l'escalier. I'm a bloated, wily honey ant,
revolted by the language nectar speaks.
Yes, sometimes surrender's the only way in,

but how to tip your ashes into rankest space?

> *Forget that, son; tell me how my daughters*
> *fare in the place of carpet snakes?*

iii.

> *Are your sisters known to the guards*
> *of King Street, whom even the cane toads shun?*
> *Or stranded by the crystal tide that surged*
> *as you honed your thees and thous*
> *upon the Bridge of Sighs and Pont Marie?*
>
> *I fear I glimpsed my daughters among the thousands*
> *of beached sea stars, when the rain tempo*
> *went haywire at Ben-Ewa—please check*
> *for gasping starfish in your latest train poem;*
> *note any resemblance to the punch leeches pack …*

Here a crown-of-thorns begins to suckle
at your temple. We hear it slurp each speckle.

iv.
Keener than a gecko's insult,
sharper than a swerve of lorikeets
roiling drunk in glucose stink—

grief is a glinting labour. Toil reeks
from aspirants to equanimity.
Wait, is this Coonowrin's or Loki's tree?

Deception Bay or Circular Quay? In time
we come to where the cruel foam
scrawls its obsessive cursive; my antique 'I'

pipes down before the lace forum
of the sea. Mum, if you're on this shore,
your painter is an expert camoufleur.

~

In turn each sister hoists her
handful to the eastern island.

The carpet snakes compose another hiss,
sizing up the nereids aslant.

Dad's stuck on the way the waves
refuse to quit, like ensnared tails.

~

Whelk-grit clings to the months' weave.
Here is here, elsewhere's elsewhere,
says monsieur obvious during a wet shave

weeks later. Well, we're all elsewhere
now, Mum. Of course the tide rushed in
to delete the glyphs our heels were

grooving, even as the grey nurse hid
you in her ancient lidless eye,
the kind of eye that could hide urns.

v.

                         Nothing else yields
quite like coastal wind as it receives ash.
As if it said, *Yes, I'll seed*

the future, as soon as your shiver ceases.
The monks had a word for it: *esssse*,
a breath that through the face's sieve arches

like an escapee porpoise, convinced it possesses
the property of those particles
whose vanishing, only, the physicist assesses.

On the return flight I watched as a sail crept
west toward the salt-marsh inlets
across an acre that shone, an escarp lit

with phosphorescence. I strained to listen

above the engines, struggled to reconcile fens
with islands. This is how khaki tinsel

dwindles: with distances that confer silence
on even the most dour falconer,
waiting by the wallum's inflorescence.

Magnifera

Ripeness was a semitone below
the bone clef of the elbow

keying the rain-slicked
cyclone fence: the firm, saclike rind

of a warped minim, golden
drupe note for which we longed.

Stone fruit are fine tutors.
This one unseals a sensual nose hit.

At dusk they go lambent
like chunks of bent gloam.

Sucked, their fibrous pith
is birth-pouf—

punk oblong pits
belonging in a goblin's pot,

infused with rich static
and the fresh electric scratchiti

of summer lightning. It's fortune
gave us this softer unit,

surely. Edgewise the frangipani
made a rain-gap fin

for heads rife with fire
in the shade of the mango belt.

Intel Fresco

I. BIOMETRICS

The gist of the signal
that breaks through the mizzle aligns

        with the singular tone
        of the note

on your file. Our almagest
tells us you live by the alms gate

        like a pent rat,
and panic when you can't discern
        a pattern
        in the cinders

of your hearth. Take these rice spoons
and join the procession.

Soon the crack search
        team is due to return
with word from the Turner-
        esque arches,

        whorls and loops
of your index and thumb, the isobars
        the air boss
draws to mimic weather on your skin.

Keeping calm will help you as we sink
        this weighted conker

        to reckon
the rich cryptical pools

of your irises; writ small
        in ripples, radial, still warm

with the first heat of creation,
        vital details
shrink and then are lost
        when your pupil dilates.

Compliance is the simplest reaction.
No, it's nothing like the slots—

it's neither chance, nor competition,
        nor a ruse,
and we don't depict emotion
        even when it juts,

but any moment now
        we'll know for sure,
        old chum,
whether you've zeroed or won

        and by just
        how much.

2. FLIGHT PATH

A stowaway ... believed to have been clinging to a British Airways
flight from Johannesburg to Heathrow ... was found on the roof of
notonthehighstreet.com's headquarters on Kew Road, Richmond ...
There have been other cases where stowaways have fallen to their
deaths in London after smuggling themselves onto planes and hiding
in landing gear.

—BBC News, 19 June 2015

It's raining men in Richmond upon Thames.
Our talk is of the latest of them as

we queue for kale smoothies. A posher atomism,
this, than that man's metamorphosis.

He hammered on a roof by Richmond Green
to be let in; wary of the unfamiliar genre

the paramedics at their shiftwork scaled
       the headquarters of the artisanal
gift store, but were without a rain atlas
       to place him. Now the motivational decals

frosted on the glass read like sorry denials—
     CHOOSE A LIFE LESS ORDINARY;
BE YOURSELF EVERYONE ELSE IS ALREADY
     TAKEN. This is a real day.

Above the High Street's summer dioramas,
did he twist like a samaroid
seed, or whistle like a samurai sword,
swiftly and without words?

3. BOUNCER

Then   trampoline
             into ampler   air,

an   opt-in realm   where
             airmen plot
to be   more pliant.

4. REMEMBRANCE DAY 2017

*Met sources said the use of the technology at the showpiece
central London event is a trial, and not related to terrorism
or serious crime. Officers have compiled a dataset of about
50 individuals … Automated facial recognition cameras will be
used to identify any individual on the list …*
                    —*The Guardian*, 11 November 2017

Live coverage, lit by not one patch
            of actual sunlight. A hot pecan
hisses from a drain beside the Cenotaph.

Each time we spin back to this spot
            in our ellipse, the Last Post
bloats with correspondence from the silent.

Today it is our plan to re-enlist
            you, the survivors, in our surveillance
scheme, that all the unclear lives

might be illuminated; though of the threads
        we've lately learned to parse
to pin things down, yours might be the hardest

        to unlace: silver
glinting breasts could drive the recognition
        software spare.

We won't encroach upon your inner cogito.

We'd like to leave you be with the silent force
        of your reflections—

        but this unusually large
        gathering in regal glare

makes for one hell of an historic intel fresco.

Carousel

Dense night is a needs thing.

You were lured
    in a luminous canoe
said to have once ruled
    a lunar ocean.

The 2 am soda pour
of stars is all but silent;
    only listen—

    sedate as a sauropod
      in the bone epics
it spills all the moon spice,

      releasing a sap odour
         that laces
      us to a vaster scale
         of road opus.

A carousel of oral cues,
these spinning sonic coins.

A slide show of old wishes.

Hard Water

Tristan's Ascension

i.m. *Blaise*

i.

The supersonic winds of Neptune might
thrum like this: one billion miles of naught

then whang: the skipping rope at warp speed
in your chest. The custom drum kit of a millipede.

ii.

Drummer boy, we know nothing of equilibrium.
But if you catch that air bubble from
the gulp of the waiting room's water cooler

you will rise like the drowned in Bill Viola
up through the roof of the sonogram
and join us in the sunroom.

iii.

Oh, son. You stepped off one stop too soon.
Your mother has flown

all the way to Titan
to look for you. She bellows to a mound

of electric sand
for a sound, one sound—

or a way to rewind
waterfalls, and rain.

Yes. We will pick you up again, again.

Hossegor

*... a high surf fell upon the shore; a more dreadful one I have
not often seen: no European boat could have landed in it ...*
                              —Joseph Banks, *Journal* (Tahiti, 29 May 1769)

Surfing probably didn't occur to the Vikings
    but then you never know—maybe one of Asgeir's men
        found himself oaring his chieftain's faering

for this Biscay shore, just as a set wave jacked—
    the kind that narrows the eyes of the guns
        who yearly light up the Quiksilver Pro

(Slater, Fanning, Medina, Florence, Parko)—
    and intuiting to lean down the face of the monster
        felt it take, the shove as the hull slotted flush

into the vein of the sea god, frisson pitching through
    the crew like the shudder of a brained seal
        as they fluked the drop on an outside bomb.

You can almost see them now, rolling in from
    out the back like hoons on a banana boat,
        on course to plough through locals. A Nerf howls

to a thud; a kitesurfer eats it. And there must
    have been some among the numberless wrecked
        who happened to cling to jetsam felicitously warped—

the waterlogged panel of a walnut armoire, say—
    as to hitch them a lift in the home stretch
        of this crumbling A-frame's deep Atlantic fetch.

Perhaps one of them even cottoned on
    that after breathing the art lies in the reading
        of the break, getting to grips with tide-shift

and how the wind's caprice vexes the take-off,
    the fickle line-up—but who among them
        could have envisioned a Tahitian king, carving?

The guns will return, who are now braving
    the skull-crushing torque of Teahupo'o.

Hard Water

The word
we used
was *mellowed*

and maybe he really had
towards the end—
but Victor took the jug cord

to the boys for years. For half a life he whirred
like a rowing machine. Barb said she heard
the grunts of effort between the strokes from her yard

across the creek; and that her bloke, Steady Brad,
as he was known before the brain bleed,
once wondered

why that effing forklift driver couldn't just unload,
until he clocked the ruckus was coming from inside
the mullet-stinking, guano-spattered

weatherboard,
two or three abandoned
Holdens further up the No Through Road.

Noosa Shane—the only Shane I know who's still loaded
now the boom has ended—
was skiing at Banksia Beach, when the semi-muffled

thuds that echoed
off the gazebo and along the promenade
spooked him, and he flooded

his flashy Suzuki four-stroke outboard.
Then there's Carol, who sometimes sleeps in the hide
in the wetlands. She reckoned

some native bird
responded
to the hurt in the wind

by clattering its own head
about the mud.
But Carol's also had it hard.

Chook, Buddha, Wayne, Stink and Rod
rarely conferred,
and even when they did they talked

around it: Rod sailed closest when he recalled
Vic's trawler in dry dock at Spinnaker Sound
that night a big fist of south, upward

of sixty knots, shunted
it leeward,
free from its chucks, and they found

the boat tilted
on its port side
in its cradle, with its outriggers totalled ...

All agreed the eldest bore the brunt. Kind kid,
Jason. Before he could speak, he ferried
turtle hatchlings on a raft of cast-off chipboard,

bridging his back against a frigate bird—
but the knock-off crowd
at Bluey's twelve years later barely blinked

up from their schooners when Vic cranked
up *What a Wonderful World*
on the jukebox and cracked

his firstborn square in the jaw with the dartboard.
Jace told me once that every time he flinched
his eyes would shut unwillingly, and a strange breed

of angel would appear, who power-lunged ahead
in him, like a nine-ironed cane toad
strumming the harp of its innards. He chaired

the rough proceedings; his instinct was to shield
the younger two, so he hogged
the conch for himself, refused to yield

his time on the floor. It rarely worked.
The second lad
now lives in Chermside,

is twice divorced,
inseparable from his dogs, Sinbad
and Hector, and hardly ever wets the bed.

The youngest I know well. He tried
so hard
to watch his fucking mouth he went cross-eyed

as he shivered in the shed.
So Vic turned optometrist, measured
the spite of each sharp clip across the void

to reset the dials on the poor bastard.
His thick glasses make him look a bit weird,
but I'm proud

of my stepdad, who I call Dad,
who finally ended it, and who probably only ended
his brief church speech when he shared

all this with me later, long after he had belted
me blue for the last time. I was reminded
of it this weekend

when I saw him reach behind the bread
and casually plug the cord
into the wall socket, the way it was intended,

while he bubbled
up with pride
about the Broncos, who had

never finished
dead
last on the ladder, and the hard water roiled.

The Longman–Dickson Axis
for the ALP

Do you hear the factory music
above the power generator?
If you answered *yes*, you're lying.
They are the same thing.

Note the soundtrack in the bite
of the bandsaw, the angle grinder.
Time and space are one
within the triggered nail gun,

while the silences between
are gripped by classic soft rock:
More Than a Feeling,
(Everything I Do) I Do It for You.

Ladybugs

Your sister etches rain into her skin.
She calibrates the weight of every nick
and then experiments with aquatint
to keep her precious hyphens out of sight.

A paperclip can be a javelin.
The scissors beckon her with open arms.
Yet mostly she prefers the safety pin
she keeps beside the ironed uniforms.

She coaxes ladybugs into the light
from some dark garden thriving in her vein,
as though she were cajoling razor clams
the way her aunties taught her at Yeppoon.

They hatch like fire opals from a vault.
They drip like crimson sequins from a gown.
You know there is a language in the welt
that lifts a pinkish lip to greet each cut,

though nobody can read the cuneiform
she chisels in the tablet of her pelt.
The primitive calligraphy won't scan—
but if you had to parse the hailstorm

you'd say it was her prep for an exam
on how to use her skin to hoard the rain,
and navigate a blazing hinterland
without a map, a mother, or a phone.

Mister Michelin

Mrs Allen was fond of discipline.
Around the time of our class projects on fossilisation,
she gave an unscheduled lesson

on the New Order: three matt-black straps, one for each
of the blind mice, fitted with hardwood handles
that had been jigsawed and sanded,

so she said, by an unnamed man friend.
Between the cursive flashcards
and the choose-your-own-adventure books, they hung

like docile eels, from designated hooks.
The first resembled the flaps that brush your suitcase
at customs, like you see on *Border Security*.

It was relatively okay, though it had a nasty way
of whipping around your hip
and stinging your special place. The next was more

like a slice of the conveyor belt itself. Its greater heft
gave you more lift, and was the go-to
for breaking bounds or playing spin the bottle.

But the last was special: a fillet of 4x4 off-road tyre,
thicker than *The Hobbit*, and warm as Smaug.
Mister Michelin seemed absurd.

He looked almost impossible to wield. And he never
was, of course: it was enough to hover
as idea; the rest we could solve with algebra.

And so, those nights, we found ourselves pursued
by a great wall of tread, zags of black lightning that said,
I was made for a monster truck. I boss clay

and mud, and I'm here to do a doughnut on your butt.
Later that term, as we sweltered in the chapel
pretending to sing *Friends are very special people,*

Saint Hilda burst forth from her dull glass panel,
and with a glance froze all the eels to stone,
along with Mrs Allen's superannuation plan.

Tips for Managing Subsidence
for Emma

One's aptitude for monitoring cracks
can be refined. This is something I learned
observing the surveyor's calipers.

Before he could decline our tea, he'd clued:
at fault was the insistence of a root—
the hawthorn in our quiet neighbour's yard—
as if some soil-blind striver, ravenous,
were headbutting the floor to thieve our juice.

'A rule of thumb,' he said. 'Let no tree grow
taller than its distance from the house.'

I have news for him. The crack is worse.
There, where the black sclerotic vein
slithers up the post and along the beam
toward the disconnected smoke alarm,
it flares into a seam of emptiness
so broad it's what the Cornish call a *zawn*.

And one more thing: my wife is rock-rimmed
in the chasm. At least, that's my best guess.

The month we lost our boy, I found her knelt
before that cold arrested lightning in our wall,
examining the rank predacious vine.
In hindsight she was charting a route.

I haven't seen her since. But on clear nights
I train my telescope beyond the joists
and make her out:
                    ropeless, shivering, a speck

at such a reckless height it wrings my guts,
free-soloing the sheer face of our loss
without a carabiner for the crux;

and squinting through the hail of scree, I glimpse
a figure arching back—to say *goodbye*?—

then racking herself once more to span the fracture,

her crimson fingers jammed
in the crevasse,

            a shape diminishing in clouds of chalk.

Bach to the Fuchsia

In thrall to thresholds, drawn to every brink,
        at three weeks old
an infant's eye adores the frames of things,
        the joinery that holds
each smudge in place, and individuates.

It feasts on edges, architraves and jambs,
        the skirting boards
of portals, vistas, stairs—the sinews of
        a monochrome Matisse
above the couch—a rim of tortoiseshell

that clasps a lens—jawlines, bevels, hems.
        Collecting motley
verges, most of all, it relishes the glinting
        blade of gold
that flashes in the gaps between the blinds

(a second birth, a scimitar aflame, that fattens
        on each careless
ghost of wind)—as if it knew the brilliant
        strip contained
some future-proof technology for life.

The leavings of a star have cast this spell,
        summoning blood
and chlorophyll—and so, the summer
        of his birth, I find myself
orbiting the block, hammering our bond

in the forge of an inhuman heatwave.
        I emphasise the hip-
jolt of each step, to simulate the rocking
        of the womb, as if
I knew. My crude technique appears to do

the trick—that glassy stare, as though he hailed
        from a pond of jellied
frogspawn, his visa from the commonwealth
        of zonk. I am a roving
gum, and this koala is my son. His pupils rowing

back toward the main, weary of their cargo,
        shove off their oars
and drift onto a eucalyptus reef, as kerbside
        fuchsias, wilting in a kiln
of scorching bitumen, collapse in heaps

of silk and taffeta upon the street like lurid
        ballerinas on the nod,
the victims of a batch of iffy pills. Back home,
        some Bach to help us
both relax, Partita No. 2 but on the lute—and as

the plucked notes run, I learn to count the cost
        my gaze extracts—how
every glance beseeches him to concentrate
        on me, the toll it takes to hew
a face from scratch and animate the world.

There There

Fort Dada

Once off the ship from sector blah blah
she checks into a spa in Baden-Baden,
wet air spiced with a pile of old *Who's Who*s
and warm custardy wafts of ylang ylang.
Only the new filtration system's murmur
and three perfect smiles of pawpaw.
Bowls heaped with wild mushroom couscous
suit the one girl from Wagga Wagga
who knows her rendang from her gado gado.
Bright and rare as a golden bulbul
she caught on quick, so flicked the frou-frou,
went off-piste: first tai chi, then the cha-cha.
Love's dance, though: now that was lose-lose.
They often wound up tangled in her yo-yo.
The holiday in Crete they fought like kri kri,
or way back in the early days in Woy Woy
when she went walkabout with the .22,
blood blurring loud above the never-never,
visions surely no-one else had had
(her naked papa brandishing his atlatl).
Day-to-day distress remains hush-hush
and being seen wallowing is a boo-boo—
so *Fuck you all*, she sighs, and *pooh-pooh
to the pricks sceptical of my juju* ...
Hence the spa, hence the Liszt by Lang Lang.
Autumn shook its crisping ochre pompom
when in the thermal mists of Baden-Baden
she winked back from her replica tuktuk
at old sector blah blah, and clinked *cin cin*.

Spork

Chimera native to our plastic age, crossbred ambassador
      from the planet of blur,
      both and not either or—

you are glued schism; a threat to the law of non-contradiction;
      compromise incarnate;
      quisling, turncoat, apostate;

the broker risking all for lasting truce; his foolish hopes
      for peace between the tribes;
      all the lit pipes

that constellate the blear of tearful summitry;
      the hard-won treaty
      as an affront to purity;

a firm, unequivocal rebuttal of unilateralism;
      some rogue 'warm
      wishes' from a troll farm;

a tied State of Origin; raucous applause on the floor
      of the rent chamber;
      the kids choosing to share—

and yet the cutlery of choice in war and prisons; ideal
      orienteering kit; humble
      campfire caboodle;

relief for klutzes with chopsticks; flower-of-the-foodcourt;
       perfectly accurate
       stabber of the halved apricot,

in tune with mashed roots, adept at tabouleh,
       farfalle, paella …
       Proud sheila fella!

Affable punk sphinx, with your mien of scoop,
       and your hairdo
       of stout cockatoo,

inscrutable statuette of liberty, enemy of monomania,
       standard bearer
       for hybrid vigour—

had I need of an heraldic crest, *you* would form the plume
       of polypropylene
       tufting from my helm,

for you were always a bit like me, spork:
       a *half-caste gook*,
       an incendiary Spock

beamed in by genetic monsoon and plonked down hard
       onto a patio on an island
       in Queensland

that gave the most rousing ovation to One Nation;
       a slap in Pop's face,
       who'd fought in the Pacific;

up-close physical proof of the peril, produced
    in his own
    daughter's womb.

She wanted to give him the forks, but it wasn't her nature
    to fight with her father.
    So she gave him the future.

Magic Hour, L.A.

for Luke Davies

Maze-bright, sans GPS down Fairfax
        in the Buick, when a thrash fiend
in a chrome Corvette salutes hang loose
        then flexes a burnout as he peels off
Sunset; and as the strains of Anthrax
        scatter in the wake of his goatee,
stars are smuggled in via the print
        of Wonder Woman's patriotic bikini.

Dusklit wildlife suffers no predicting:
        a lobster juggles bibles unicycling
in the poorly lit scene of his mind,
        a polymath samples his own urine,
while as on a folding screen depicting
        notable scenes in feudal Kyoto,
a buff pimp in denim cut-offs blazes
        drunk karate outside a One Hour Photo.

So we drive in silence, depending on
        A Forest by The Cure for conversation.
It's like Almendros said: magic hour
        is really only twenty-five minutes max,
when the locust sun descending on
        a field of bending wheat is prologue
to a tale stripped of all denouement,
        and silhouettes are all our dialogue.

Stagger Lee at Her Majesty's

By the sand-crab mousse   a former editor of *The Sun*
         is topping up   her flute
                  of pink champa
                                    g
                                    n
                                    e—
               an aid
               worker vows   to introduce her
                                        to Wolverine.
Naturally I fall
      in   with   the play
               wrights
               and an oddly
               foppish
                        yob from   Toowoomba
                  fluent
         in several   ocker dialects
running an ex
                     pat news   paper.
      Like salacious   columnists
                     we're in bits   just witnessing
         'The Body'   sluice
                     through   a bank of tail
            ored suits, still
                              hot as lime   juice
on a torn
cuticle,   to blithely dis miss the crab mousse—
         two decades on   from the all-out

fluorescent assault
of her work   for   Diet Coke in '88.

                              Word   wobbles   'round
            that Rolf has
                          got the   flu (ahem)
            and poor Clive   is properly
    crook: some say he watches re-runs
                                            of *The Wire*
                  over   and over.
    My patois is a heady   mix of am
                              nesia, em
                                      pire and capital

            and just
                      as I'm realising
                                            (recalling) this
    the scene shifts   to the portrait
                                      gallery, where

                              the high priest
                              of duende,

        like some jet-haired Catalan
              entrepreneur
          straight out of Velásquez,
              widens the aperture:

                        a brooding gothic currawong
                        among a froth of swans.

Surveying What Adheres

What was your status as of Monday?
Low on cling film. Fine for surface spray.

Name one highlight of your current job.
Midway on my journey to the Tube

the sticky men come tumbling down the glass
of the High Commission, a few yards

north of the Dominion. Hurled, they thwack
the tint, as though each wodge of gunk

were phlegm hoiked up from
underground, so thick it sprouted limbs.

The sticky men?
The toys I mean.

Those moulded figurines of polymer
and mucilage slash tackifier

that wobble down to Earth like a mirage.
The de facto mascots of our plastic age.

And you learned what from your sticky man phase?
Perhaps the smear of North Atlantic ooze,

the veiny blob of albumen
that Huxley once mistakenly proclaimed

the missing link
appeared to him like *this*:

expectorated sputum, anthropoid,
squished against the window of a slide.

Is there anything else you wish to add?
The finest nanotech adhesive yet

aspires to the tread
of gecko feet.

Force Majeure

Among the starlike flowers
        of the lacebark in the Sun-
corp building's garden bed,
        he met a blue-faced honeyeater
snacking on aphid sashimi.
        To gain its trust he noshed
on freshest sushi of the soil—
        an Hibiscus Harlequin beetle,
whose bright shield shone
        as he crunched it for protein.
Invoking the savage, all-too-
        permanent red lightning
of the common Jezebel's wing—
        a scarlet splash as if glassed
in a pub brawl—he whistled *woik*
        and *queet,* then saddled up
and vanished into the thin
                uninsurable air.

Wingsuit Lessons

Slipping through
        an isotherm's lasso
                we skate across
                        an icy shelf of air,
                                quick enough to lick
                                        the swiftest Yamaha.

                                        Nylon-clad we flambé

the moraine, sear
        permafrost, blister the cryosphere.

                        We scrawl our melt-
                                water signatures then
                                        puff! through a cloud of
                                                fuscous alpine moths

        leaving them cartoonishly
                        dis   com
                                bob   u   la
                                                ted.

                        Fern spores
                flounder in
        the eddies
of our boom carpet manoeuvres.

We hug gorges,
        gouge huge sockets
                of stone, scraping the nappe
                        with flared wingtips.

87

Fanatical clerics
of adrenaline
        we stocktake the infinite
        Swiss mist,
        accounting for each warehouse in a
        blink,

then buzz the picnickers beside the dip
    into the poplar run
        with our terrible swoop:

a pissed-off Apollo, deciduous Daphne, a horrible picture
    of insistence, the willingness
        to risk annihilation
            for the thing that most interests us,

the ravishment of gravity. They are frightened
            out of their jumpsuits
            by the velocity of our zoom

    and forget it is only
a sophisticated kind of falling.

    To fly we'd have to be
        like any winged insect:

        able to calculate
            our coefficient of lift
                relative to the wind

                    instinctively.

One hot pocket can knock you into a spin
          and then you're smeared, glistening
in the cliff with the fossilised coral,
          the dressing on a Holocene salad.

So make of your hand an edge to knife the air,
          like this, and now your arm
               an oar with which to split
                    the fiercest river of wind.

Do not attempt to sing; your voice
is commandeered by the massif. Lastly,

               be like Syrinx and make your body
                  lyrical—
               all your song is in the line you take
               when buzzing the jagged peak.

Go now. If you want me I'll be scoping
          the keyhole in the gneiss.

On Not Getting My Spray Can Signed
by Mr Brainwash

after Elvis (2009), by Thierry Guetta

It's not that I'd prefer
    another portrait of St Michael
to Elvis wielding an M16
    designed by Fisher & Paykel.

Wait, I mean by Fisher-Price—
    point being I appreciate
a top-shelf Invader piece
    as much as any Eurydice,

and I'm pretty sure I get
    the way our fetishisation
of the toy assault rifle
    inflects his canonisation

as The King. It's just that capital
    encourages this: the endless
permutations of its effects
    are hardly less mindless.

The hubris is in thinking
    of each meme-savvy mashup
as a protest, allied to a flash
    mob trashing Topshop.

It's not. This canvas is passive
        as TV. No caulking with irony
can prevent its schtick's hull
        ripping on the reef of cliché.

I pray to Duchamp not to be
        the guy who cries *Scheissers!*
unfazed that he's conscripted
        by the thing he criticises.

Below the Line

Once off the ship from sector blah blah
          <<snip snip>>

personfromporlock wrote at 23:55:
                              Yeah yeah.
What started out so-so
quickly became the same old, same old—
          really just another *there there*
number, parading the ghost of his mama,

          nostalgic for the promise of Expo '88,
longing for the turquoise lagoons of Bora Bora,
where *flash as sailfish, headstrong as mahi-mahi,*
muscular as leaping marlin, I ... yadda yadda.

You know, the usual. Can't say I took it in *in*

                                        toto.
What I did read reminded me of the Berber
          I bunked with in Woop Woop
during my gap years—the faintly musical *donk donk*
of the goat bells. Sure it was funny, but not ha-ha

funny; more funny-sad, like the elegy for Ford Ford
in William Williams's *The Wedge* ('44).
Or the porcelain sunflower seeds of Ai WeiWei.

In a dream we're onstage at Hay-on-Wye, Ai and I. I
          play the spectral glide, the wah-wah
rhythm to his laser beam. Pew pew.

'Something's up with this game's AI,' Ai
mutters, hurling his console. 'Aye yai yai,
          Ai,' I cry, dodging. 'Watch it, ya big dodo!'

          'Pedantry's a gateway drug! Ask John Lyly!'
          shouts a heckler in—is it Gubbi Gubbi?

And I would've asked him too, but ... But
what? But Lyly was at the putt putt
practising his trick shots with Boutros Boutros

          Ghali, Lady Gaga,
          Gigi
and one of the Durans from Duran Duran.
                    I know I know,
          there were no actual Durans in Duran Duran,

but what work doesn't leak? Like the sly drip drip
against the party leader at a bunga bunga,

art is deep background, a rumoured fifty-fifty
fuck between knack and technique, the glug glug
of Bob Hawke with a yard glass, and the inevitable tsk tsk.

admin wrote at 00:00:
Stop, thief! What's the big idea? That's *my* tutu.

Coloratura
i.m. Clive Hart (1931–2016) and Bernard Hickey (1931–2007)

Said the Australian Joycean
to no-one especially: 'I find my heart, and my nation
where I most and least expect:
a yellow-labelled jar of yeast extract;

the apostrophe lost in the infinity pool
of *Finnegans Wake*; the obscenity trial

of ~~Kylie's hotpants; Dame Joan's coloratura; Angus Young for mooning
Illinois; Michael Hutchence's death by autoerotic asphyxiation; the
Steve Irwin episode of South Park; the inventor of the black box;
Les Murray that time at Magdalen College explaining what a camel
toe was to the embarrassed fellows and twittering undergrads really
labouring the point and then going off on a tangent about the dark
web and all the nasty~~ "Nausicaa";

thirty Dodge Chargers in the NASCAR
Elite Division,
flicking ignition and roaring in unison
at Thunderdome. Hmmm,
I guess I really am like Leopold Bloom.'

'The number of fools is infinite,'
replied the man from Eccles Street,
citing Augustine
citing Ecclesiastes,
but not the famous bit about there being nothing new under the sun.

References

[1] thunder apes
father

[2] rain quotes
mother

[3] lightning cites
the child

Crookneck
(Coonowrin)

Husband, mountain, cooled volcanic
remnant, come. We may be stuck as magma plugs, but can it
really be so hard to turn and look upon your son?

Here is his soiled exercise book. See how the acreage of each
page is rich to the edge with geometric formulae, a sea of
pineapples; and there, scribbled in sclerophyll, scratched in
sugar cane, your chip, your kin, rehearsing his signature.

These million years he's only known the blue slab of your back;
is fluent in its nuances, in fact, and can decode your mood from
the smoulder of your lats. He reads the slightest flicker in your
traps, idolises your tatts.

Forget about that business with the flood. He never meant to
be so slow to help. I acknowledge the wallop seems to have
done him good.

Like I say: I know we are rock, but seeing as once you snapped
his neck, surely you could break the laws of physics again
and pay him some attention.

> It would mean the world
> if you could
>
> take a quick
> squiz at his homework.

Coonowrin
(Crookneck)

Hushbound, mountchain, coiled for-kin ache
revenant, calm. Warm hay be stark enigma flags, but cannot
rarely be sore heart to tune and luck upon your sighin'?

Hairy seas oiled exorcise bark. Sea haw the anchorage of itch
purges wretch demiurge wit sheer tragic ululae, lease of pain
armfuls; ends air, scrabbled in clear offal, squinched insurgent
coin, u-shape, ur-chain, rehashing is songnature.

Thief zillion ears he's songly none the blur slob of your beak;
is fluenz in its noiances, infect, and cairn de-God our mud frame
the smelter of your salts. He weeds the slidest flee Göring your
traipse, idylllazes your stats.

Fogged apart sat bees nice weather fled. He naïver mentor
bezels low to gulp. Aye rock-ledge, the whelp sums to weave
downhill cloud.

Lark eyes, hey: ignoble earruck, obscening in sense you sniped
inuksuk, surly you cold brook the lows of viz-aches agon
imply hymn same intention.

> It word mine the whorled
> if Euclid
>
> torque a quark
> squeeze as his dreamwoke.

Cinemetabolic

i.

Hiera that gufforging in the popcorn bushes?

Who gopher, wearing my super money under plans
on 'is nonce, mummering in backhards elvish,
slobbering on gin jeering cinememe eye creme?

Methinks you seem a phantasthma, I heed
you breathink, it sussurounded golden rough.
Shake my handvice, nevermind this placenomore,

you shld quid it at ones. Snow write for you.
Belong you beyond the starpark, long wayfare
these pumpkin Bosches. Less faith it, y'aint

cart hut for these kinds of sillygigs; these pleading
shenanicairns can girt too mush laughter a while,
heaven for thus of us whore eucharist.

ii.

Theuth, haranguer of diction. Shore, hive
bean cauled ah word-shipper of falls codes
on a cunt of mire pen chant phwoar ludicism—

sewed watt? Joist beakers eye plague wist whirrs
dozen meek mean ember seal no doze it,
hoar son short of Charlie Tan Hu dozing

no wow to strum a signdance to get her?
Stare a money ovums who luck to murk a run
wide long wedge. An wart elles cairn wee

caul hour sell wheelie phut—yelp, use gassed it—
bowettes, for womb plaiting wit worlds hints away
orph peeing. Strewth, rearrange my ear action.

iii.
Too nigh: woe grimes in the cous cous cous,
the mass of cars in hommus; the untied stays
of asparagus kendo no think while rasher

and try nah twiddle their tombs inshifting on
their shove reign tea. Eye must say I dis écrit
whip the polyp seas webbed up hover whizz quay

baht zen ark hen zaps duh whey beers 'n' ears
his dun thief daze, oar a till east sow eye herd.
Whey cup, hits thyme two hacked, fours arse

ache hoof hour crate cram shelled wren,
hand haul off there shelled wren to calm.

Notes

The epigraph is from John Harris's *Lexicon Technicum, Or, An Universal English Dictionary of Arts and Sciences,* vol. 1 (London: Brown, Goodwin et al., 1704).

'ROTFLMAOWTRDMF': Nekhtnebf (also Nekhtnebef, Gr. Nectanebo I) was the founder of the XXX Dynasty (380–343 BCE), the last native dynasty of Ancient Egypt, which ended when his nephew, Nekhtharheb (Gr. Nectanebo II), fled the Persian army led by Artaxerxes III. Some sources suggest Nekhtharheb was the grandson (rather than nephew) of Nekhtnebf; this poem follows more recent analysis of the inscription on the sculpture of Nekhtharheb's father at the Metropolitan Museum of Art, *The General Tjahapimu* (360–343 B.C.) (Gallery 128), which indicates he was the *brother* (not the son) of Nektnebf (making Nekhtharheb the latter's *nephew*). This is discussed on The Met's website entry for the item.

'Rimbaud in Salatiga' is inspired by accounts of Arthur Rimbaud's voyage to Java in the second half of 1876, in Graham Robb's *Rimbaud: A Biography* (Picador, 2000) and Jamie James's *Rimbaud in Java: The Lost Voyage* (Didier Millet, 2011). The epigraph by Yves Bonnefoy is quoted in Robb, p. 290. The phrases 'archipelagos of stars' and 'million golden birds' are from 'The Drunken Boat' (*Le Bateau ivre*), in Arthur Rimbaud, *Collected Poems*, trans. Oliver Bernard (Baltimore: Penguin Books, 1962), p. 170.

'Mirrigin' is the word for 'stars' in the Turrubal-Yagera language of Brisbane and South East Queensland, according to Tom

Petrie's lexicon in Constance Campbell Petrie, *Tom Petrie's Reminiscences of Early Queensland*, first published in 1904 (UQP, 1994, p. 323). The poem refers to two notorious massacres of Aboriginal people through the poisoning of flour by European settlers: one at Kilcoy Station in 1842, and another at Whiteside in Moreton Bay in 1847.

'The Nothing' takes its epigraph from *The NeverEnding Story*, written and directed by Wolfgang Petersen, 1984.

'パックマン Études': the first word of the title is Japanese (*katakana*) for *Pac-Man* (created by Toru Iwatani in 1980). The hybrid Japanese–French title translates as 'Pac-Man Studies'.

'Citicity' takes its title and epigraph from Richard Brown, 'Time, Space and the City in "Wandering Rocks"', *European Joyce Studies 12: Joyce's 'Wandering Rocks'*, edited by Andrew Gibson and Steven Morrison (Amsterdam: Rodopi Press, 2002), p. 59.

'A Nice Derangement of Epitaphs' takes its title from Richard Sheridan's 1775 play *The Rivals*.

'You Hear It Said' refers to two instructional books: Ted Hughes's *Poetry in the Making* (London: Faber, 2008), pp. 58–61; and Fiona Sampson's *Poetry Writing: The Expert Guide* (London: Robert Hale, 2009), pp. 92–3.

'Plunder (Business as Usual)' takes the parenthetical portion of its title, and its epigraph, from the 1981 Men at Work album, *Business as Usual*. 'Colin' is Colin Hay, the band's Scottish-Australian lead vocalist.

The poems in the second part, 'Biometrics', are all composed in an invented form, which uses anagrams in place of rhyme (e.g. 'water mint' / 'am written' / 'winter mat').

'The Convict Lying Low by Hampton Court, Speaks': 'Arethusa'—the Arethusa fountain in Bushy Park, the second largest of London's Royal Parks. Now known as the Diana Fountain, it is the centrepiece of Sir Christopher Wren's 'approach' to Hampton Court Palace.

'Credo, Décor, Coder': 'the salted ghost of Ian'—Ian Fairweather (1891–1974), Scottish-Australian painter who in the last decades of his life resided near what is now Buckleys Hole Conservation Park on Bribie Island, Queensland. The poem refers to numerous places on the island and its surrounds, including the surfside suburb Woorim, Ben-Ewa on Moreton Island, the Glass House Mountains (Mount Tibrogargan and Mount Coonowrin) and Deception Bay. 'Place of carpet snakes' is the translation of Caboolture (from the Indigenous dialect of Gubbi Gubbi, 'Kabul-tur').

'Tristan's Ascension' takes its title from Bill Viola's six-metre-high video installation, *Tristan's Ascension (The Sound of a Mountain Under a Waterfall)* (2005).

'Hossegor': 'Asgeir'—ninth-century Viking chief and invader of Gascony, where the surf-town of Hossegor is located. Teahupo'o (in Tahiti) and Hossegor host successive events on the professional World Surf League's Championship Tour. The epigraph is from Joseph Banks's journal entry for 29 May 1769, made in Tahiti on HMS *Endeavour*, widely considered the earliest recorded observation of surfing by a European, in

Journal of the Right Hon. Sir Joseph Banks (Cambridge: Cambridge University Press, 2011), p. 93. The entry continues: 'their chief amusement was carried on by the stern of an old canoe; with this before them they swam out as far as the outermost breach, then one or two would get into it and opposing the blunt end to the breaking wave were hurried in with incredible swiftness'.

'The Longman–Dickson Axis' refers to two adjoining federal electorates, Longman and Dickson, in South East Queensland.

'Magic Hour, L.A.': 'Almendros'—Nestor Almendros (1930–92), director of photography for Terrence Malick's 1978 film *Days of Heaven*. His remarks on 'magic hour' appear in an interview with cinematographer Haskell Wexler (*Days of Heaven: Criterion Collection*, DVD, 2007).

'Surveying What Adheres': 'Huxley … missing link'—While examining a sample of albuminous ooze from the Atlantic sea floor in 1868, British biologist T.H. Huxley (1825–95) mistakenly thought he had discovered a form of primordial matter, the *Urschleim* that his contemporary, Ernst Haeckel, proposed was the source of organic life. Huxley later retracted the claim after it was disproven. 'Missing link' here refers to the transition from chemistry to biology (the origin of life), rather than its more common connotation of gaps in the fossil record.

'Coloratura' is dedicated to the memory of two Australian expatriate academics: Clive Hart, the prolific James Joyce scholar; and Bernard Hickey, who taught literature in Venice, and founded the Centre for Australian Studies in the Mediterranean at the University of Lecce.

'Coonowrin' and 'Crookneck' both concern the Indigenous Dreaming story of the Glass House Mountains in South East Queensland. During a great flood, the father, (Mount) Tibrogargan, grew incensed that his son, (Mount) Coonowrin, did not come to the aid of his mother, (Mount) Beerwah, so struck him, dislocating his neck. Local historian Gwen Trundle writes: 'Even today Tibrogargan gazes far out to sea and never looks around at Coonowrin, who hangs his head and cries, his tears running off to sea', quoted in J.G. Steele, *Aboriginal Pathways in Southeast Queensland and the Richmond River* (UQP, 1984), p. 172.

'Cinemetabolic' is inspired by the recurrent 'Mutt and Jute' episodes in James Joyce's *Finnegans Wake* (Oxford University Press, 2012), beginning with pp. 16–18.

Acknowledgements

Acknowledgements are due to the editors of the following publications in which some of these poems have appeared: *Kenyon Review, The London Magazine, Poetry* (Chicago), *Poetry Daily, Poetry International, The Poetry Review, Shearsman, This Corner, Australian Book Review, Australian Poetry Journal, The Best Australian Poems 2013, 2014, 2016, 2017* (Black Inc.), *Cordite Poetry Review, Griffith Review, Island, Marrickville Pause, Meanjin, Overland, Rabbit, Southerly, Stilts* and *The Weekend Australian*. 'Credo, Décor, Coder' was commissioned by University of Queensland Press for *Reading the Landscape: A Celebration of Australian Writing* (2018). 'Intel Fresco' appeared (as 'Biometrics') in *Wretched Strangers* (Norwich: Boiler House Press, 2018). Earlier versions of some poems in the third and fourth sections, including 'Stagger Lee at Her Majesty's' (formerly 'Nick Cave at Buckingham Palace') and 'Force Majeure' (formerly 'Act of God'), appeared in the chapbook *Maze Bright* (Sydney and Tokyo: Vagabond Press, Rare Object Series, no. 99, 2014).

I am grateful to my editor, Lisa Gorton, for her astute and generous feedback, and to Nam Le, Liam Ferney, Claire Potter, Aidan Coleman, Kate Crowcroft and Marcel Dorney for their helpful comments on the manuscript. Sincere thanks to my publisher, Aviva Tuffield, the team at UQP, and to Felicity Plunkett, for recommending this collection to the press. This book is dedicated in part to my son, Xavier, but my deepest gratitude is due to his mother, Emma. With thanks also to the Australia Council for the Arts for a residency at the Cité International des Arts, Paris, where some of these poems were written.